For

M000029398

Happy Mothers Day
2006

I love you

Shirley

Soul Retreats™

_____

Presented To

_____

Presented By

_____

Date

Soul Retreats™ for Moms
ISBN 0-310-98899-3

Copyright 2002 by GRQ Ink, Inc.
1948 Green Hills Boulevard
Franklin, Tennessee 37067

"Soul Retreats" is a trademark owned by GRQ, Inc.

Published by Inspirio™, The gift group of Zondervan
5300 Patterson Avenue, SE
Grand Rapids, Michigan 49530

Requests for information should be addressed to:
Inspirio™, The gift group of Zondervan
Grand Rapids, Michigan 49530

http://www.inspiriogifts.com

Editor and Compiler: Lila Empson
Associate Editor: Janice Jacobson
Project Manager: Tom Dean
Manuscript written and prepared by Melinda Mahand
Design: Whisner Design Group

02 03 04/HK/ 4 3 2

Soul Retreats™
for Moms

inspirio™

Contents

Introduction

At home or away, day or night, rain or shine—as a mom you are always available to meet the needs of your family with loving care. Yet where can you turn when you long for a moment of personal encouragement and understanding? Turn to one of these fifteen-minute meditations in *Soul Retreats*™ *for Moms*. You will discover uplifting reflections and insights spoken uniquely to the heart of a mom. Each meditation provides an opportunity for the burdens and the tensions of the day to drift away as you enjoy a brief time of quiet solitude and communion with the Lord.

You may browse through the meditation titles and choose each day the selection that addresses your present need, or you may prefer to simply read the meditations in the order they are printed. Either way, God will speak to your heart and restore your spirit during these special moments of Soul Retreat™.

The Hand I Know

If I were the mighty, roaring sea with waters that surge and foam,
I'd know the hand that traced the shore and set the boundaries of my home.

If I were a faraway glittering star ablaze in the nighttime sky,
I'd know the hand that fashioned the heavens and secured me proud and high.

If I were a mountain of jagged stone so tall I towered o'er the earth,
I'd know the hand that carved my form and determined its height and girth.

But I am one whom the Maker calls "child," and He is a Father to me.
So I know the hand that gently grasps mine and gives me security.

Melinda Mahand

Safe in His Arms

As you pause from the activities of your day, let your mind and your body rest for a moment. Sink into the pillows of a soft chair or couch and feel the tension leave you. As you let relaxation wrap you in comfort, think about what wonderful things you have wrapped your arms around throughout the years—perhaps a pile of spicy, new-fallen leaves, perhaps a long-missed friend, perhaps your newborn child those first precious weeks of life.

As you enjoy these memories, realize that your arms are not only the receivers of comfort and security, but they are the givers of these blessings as well. No one else can provide your children the assurance they find and the peace they experience when they are wrapped in your arms and comforted by your voice. Although your children may sometimes flex their tiny muscles to impress you, and although they may pretend to be fierce in games of make-believe, you know they would instantly run to the protective shelter of your arms if a real threat arose. They find comfort and strength in your arms.

Our great matters are little to God's infinite power,
and our little matters are great to His Father's love.
—DONALD GREY BARNHOUSE

A Moment to Reflect

God longs to be the protective arms and reassuring voice in your life. He waits for you to run to him when you need shelter, comfort, or strength. He will gently hold you in his care and speak the words your heart so desperately needs to hear: *You are safe, my child. Rest here in my arms.*

These moments of rest offer a quiet opportunity for you to talk to God. He cares deeply about the tasks and concerns that have overwhelmed your heart today. He will restore your soul as you linger in the safety of his presence and listen to the reassuring words he whispers to your heart.

The thunder rolled; the storm clouds blew.
Yet my child slept the whole night through.
Securely tucked within my arm,
She knew that she was safe from harm.

Lord, help me learn to trust in You
When storm clouds blow in my life, too.
Hold me close within Your care,
And let me find true shelter there.

❧

—MELINDA MAHAND

9

The LORD tends his flock like a shepherd:
He gathers the lambs in his arms
and carries them close to his heart;
he gently leads those that have young.

Isaiah 40:11

A Moment to Refresh

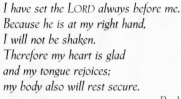

I have set the LORD always before me.
Because he is at my right hand,
I will not be shaken.
Therefore my heart is glad
and my tongue rejoices;
my body also will rest secure.

Psalm 16:8–9

The eternal God is your refuge,
and underneath are the everlasting arms.

Deuteronomy 33:27

Your arm is endued with power;
your hand is strong, your right hand exalted.
Righteousness and justice
are the foundation of your throne;
love and faithfulness go before you.
Blessed are those who have learned
to acclaim you, who walk in the light
of your presence, O LORD.

Psalm 89:13–15

When you keep your face turned toward God, He will give you rest from worry and fear.

⁓

—Diane Noble

You did not receive a spirit that makes you a slave again to fear, but you received the Spirit of sonship. And by him we cry, "Abba, Father." The Spirit himself testifies with our spirit that we are God's children.
Romans 8:15–16

*Do not fear, for I am with you;
do not be dismayed, for I am your God.
I will strengthen you and help you;
I will uphold you with my righteous
right hand.*
Isaiah 41:10

*God will cover you with his feathers,
and under his wings you will find refuge;
his faithfulness will be your shield and
rampart. You will not fear the terror
of night, nor the arrow that
flies by day.*
Psalm 91:4–5

True safety is not found by one who simply runs from danger. Rather it is the joyous discovery of the soul that runs to God.

⁓

—Melinda Mahand

He Waits for You

A Moment to Pause

Today you have given your time caring for others. Just now, give a few moments back to yourself. Go to your favorite big-armed chair or sunlit table. Wait for your pace and your pulse to slow down. Let this time of quiet waiting be a gift of restoration to your soul.

Unfortunately, restoration is not the usual result of waiting in today's society. We tend to grow fidgety if we stand in a checkout line or sit in a doctor's office for even a few minutes. In our attempt to avoid waiting, we master everything from instant oatmeal to instant messages. We expect our food fast and our packages overnight. Simply put, we consider waiting to be a waste of time.

Yet God's attitude toward waiting is dramatically different from ours, for God willingly waits with patience and longsuffering toward us. Why is God waiting for us? He is waiting for us to grow up.

Just as our children were not born fully mature adults, neither were we instantly mature when first we trusted Christ. In fact, we were mere "infants in Christ" (1 Corinthians 3:1). So God our parent patiently waits and watches with expectation for signs of growth in his children.

Speaking the truth in love, we are to grow up in all aspects
into Him, who is the head, even Christ.
—EPHESIANS 4:15 NASB

A Moment to Reflect

Without anxiety, without discouragement, ask God to guide your heart as you consider your growth in Christ thus far. How far down the road to maturity have you walked?

Too often when we consider spiritual growth, we feel like complete failures, and as a result of those feelings, we give up. So today, neither focus on past failures, except to repent of them, nor focus on present successes, except to praise God for them. Focus instead on where God wants you to be tomorrow and ask him the steps to take to get there. As you read his Word and talk with him, his Spirit will guide you. Remember always that he is patiently waiting for you to learn the way.

Gradual growth in grace, growth in knowledge, growth in faith, growth in love, growth in holiness, growth in humility, growth in spiritual-mindedness—all this I see clearly taught and urged in Scripture, and clearly exemplified in the lives of many of God's saints. But sudden, instantaneous leaps from conversion to consecration I fail to see in the Bible.

—J. C. Ryle

LORD, you are like a shield that keeps me safe.
You help me win the battle. Your strong right
hand keeps me going. You bend down to make
me great.

Psalm 18:35 NIV

A Moment to Refresh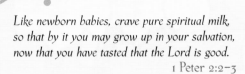

Like newborn babies, crave pure spiritual milk,
so that by it you may grow up in your salvation,
now that you have tasted that the Lord is good.

1 Peter 2:2–3

Grow in the grace and knowledge of our Lord
and Savior Jesus Christ. To him be glory both
now and forever!

2 Peter 3:18

My friends, keep on building yourselves up on
your most sacred faith. Pray in the power of the
Holy Spirit, and keep yourselves in the love of
God, as you wait for our Lord Jesus Christ in
his mercy to give you eternal life.

Jude 20–21 GNT

Happy is he who makes daily progress and who considers not what he did yesterday but what advance he can make today.

—JEROME

Continue to work out your salvation with fear and trembling, for it is God who works in you to will and to act according to his good purpose.

Philippians 2:12–13

The righteous will flourish like a palm tree.

Psalm 92:12

Do not ignore this one fact, beloved, that with the LORD one day is like a thousand years, and a thousand years are like one day. The LORD is not slow about his promise, as some think of slowness, but is patient with you, not wanting any to perish, but all to come to repentance.

2 Peter 3:8–9 NRSV

Our ground of hope is that God does not weary of mankind.

—RALPH W. SOCKMAN

Mirror Images

A Moment to Pause

Are you ready for a break today? Stop for these few moments and quietly reflect on the woman who helped mold who you are, how you think, what you believe, and how you behave. Do you know who that woman is? Of course, she is your mother.

Your mother's influence was deeply imbedded in your heart when you were just a child. She influenced your character, your values, your thoughts, your beliefs, and your behaviors. Although you are now an adult, this influence sometimes bubbles unexpectedly to the surface, and you suddenly recognize your mother's reflection in your words or actions. Perhaps you have chuckled as you recalled one of these instances to a friend. Perhaps you have even secretly felt grateful to see the family resemblance.

Likewise, as a dearly loved child of God, the Lord's influence becomes deeply imbedded in your heart. He molds who you are, how you think, what you believe, and how you behave. As you grow to reflect more and more of him, he gives you the privilege of being his mirror image to the world. You are actually invited to imitate him!

*Be imitators of God, therefore,
as dearly loved children.*
—EPHESIANS 5:1

A Moment to Reflect

When your life begins to reflect the heavenly Father, it benefits you, and it gives God pleasure. Yet equally as important is what his reflection offers to the world. As his child, you have an amazing opportunity to let people glimpse what God is like. Your life becomes a physical demonstration of God's love and power to those who do not know him. He uses your example and your testimony to draw people to him.

Thank God today for this awesome privilege. Commit to grow more in his image each day. Imagine how pleased he will be when his influence comes bubbling to the surface and you begin to imitate him. Think how he will delight to see the family resemblance.

I would be true, for there are those who trust me;
I would be pure, for there are those who care;
I would be strong, for there is much to suffer;
I would be brave, for there is much to dare.

I would be prayerful, through each busy moment;
I would be constantly in touch with God.
I would be tuned to hear His slightest whisper;
I would have faith to keep the path Christ trod.

—Howard Al Walter

17

*Try to be at peace with everyone, and try to live
a holy life, because no one will see the LORD
without it.*

Hebrews 12:14 GNT

A Moment to Refresh

*You are Light in the Lord; walk as children of
Light (for the fruit of the Light consists in all
goodness and righteousness and truth), trying
to learn what is pleasing to the Lord.*

Ephesians 5:8–10 NASB

*Remember your leaders, who spoke the word of
God to you. Consider the outcome of their way
of life and imitate their faith.*

Hebrews 13:7

*God has chosen you, because our gospel came
to you not simply with words, but also with
power, with the Holy Spirit and with deep
conviction. You know how we lived among you
for your sake. You became imitators of us and
of the Lord; in spite of severe suffering, you
welcomed the message with the joy given by the
Holy Spirit. And so you became a model to all
the believers.*

1 Thessalonians 1:4–7

Where one reads the Bible, a hundred read you and me.

—D. L. Moody

May our Lord Jesus Christ himself and
God our Father, who loved us and in his
grace gave us unfailing courage and a firm
hope, encourage you and strengthen you to
always do and say what is good.
2 Thessalonians 2:16–17 GNT

My dear friend, do not imitate what is bad,
but imitate what is good. Whoever does
good belongs to God.
3 John 11 GNT

Let the word of Christ dwell in you richly
as you teach and admonish one another
with all wisdom, and as you sing psalms,
hymns and spiritual songs with gratitude in
your hearts to God. And whatever you do,
whether in word or deed, do it all in the
name of the Lord Jesus, giving thanks to
God the Father through him.
Colossians 3:16–17

*The Christian is
called to be the
partner of God in
the conversion of
men.*

—William Barclay

A Mighty Fortress

A Moment to Pause

Where is your favorite place to take a break, to hide for a few brief moments from the demands of the day? Go there now. Enjoy the sanctuary this place offers your body and your mind.

The contentment you feel at having your own special place to hide from the world begins at a young age. How often has your child come to you for refuge, curled in your lap, nestled in your arms, or snuggled by your side?

A relationship with someone who protects you, someone who makes you feel safe, someone in whose presence you can hide is a blessing nothing else in life can replace. Your soul craves such security. Thus God may have blessed you with a parent, spouse, or friend through whom he works to help fulfill that need.

Yet discovering that another human being cannot completely fulfill your need for security does not take long. As a mom, you recognize that the battles of life loom large, the pain of losing is deep, and the aftereffects of the assault are long lasting. So today God offers you a mighty fortress, a place of refuge. He is your shelter, your rock, your hiding place in all the battles of life.

Thou art my hiding place and my shield,
O Lord: I hope in thy word.
—*Psalm 119:114 KJV*

A Moment to Reflect

Historically, the fortress was not only a place where people were safe, but it was also a place where provisions were stored. Food and water, weaponry, and medical supplies were all housed within its walls.

Likewise, God not only offers you a place of security, but he also offers a place of provision. In him you will discover nourishment, and the strength life requires, weaponry for the battles life entails, and healing for the wounds life inflicts.

Remember too that a fortress was almost always built around a town. It was not simply a place for retreat when threats loomed; it was a place to live. Choose just now to live in God's provision and protection, for true security is found ultimately in him alone.

Be still my soul: the Lord is on thy side;
Bear patiently the cross of grief or pain;
Leave to thy God to order and provide;
In every change he faithful will remain.
Be still, my soul: thy best, thy heavenly friend
Through thorny ways leads to a joyful end.

—*Katharina Van Schlegel*
(*from Psalm 46:10*)

God is our refuge and strength, an ever-present help in trouble.
Therefore we will not fear, though the earth give way
and the mountains fall into the heart of the sea.

Psalm 46:1–2

A Moment to Refresh

It is the LORD who goes before you. He will be
with you; he will not fail you or forsake you.
Do not fear or be dismayed.

Deuteronomy 31:8 NRSV

The LORD is my rock,
my fortress and my deliverer;
my God is my rock, in whom I take refuge,
my shield and the horn of my salvation.
He is my stronghold, my refuge and my savior.

2 Samuel 22:2–3

The salvation of the righteous
comes from the LORD;
he is their stronghold in time of trouble.
The LORD helps them and delivers them;
he delivers them from the wicked
and saves them, because they take
refuge in him.

Psalm 37:39–40

Rock of ages, cleft for me, let me hide myself in Thee.

—AUGUSTUS M. TOPLADY

We who have this spiritual treasure are like common clay pots, in order to show that the supreme power belongs to God, not to us. We are often troubled, but not crushed; sometimes in doubt, but never in despair; there are many enemies, but we are never without a friend; and though badly hurt at times, we are not destroyed.

2 Corinthians 4:7–9 GNT

How great is your goodness, O Lord, which you have stored up for those who fear you, which you bestow in the sight of men on those who take refuge in you. In the shelter of your presence you hide them from the intrigues of men; in your dwelling you keep them safe from accusing tongues.

Psalm 31:19–20

What is the rock within which the heart of man can safely live? Has it been named? Has it not been called the Rock of Ages? And have not they who have fled to it been assured day by day of ever-increasing security? That rock is open to us all. Blessed are they who flee to it that they may find rest and sustenance.

—JOSEPH PARKER

A Word You Need

A Moment to Pause   Crickets chirping beneath a star-filled sky, waves rushing toward a sandy shore, birds singing in a sparkling fountain—some sounds in nature have an amazing capacity to soothe our minds and restore our souls. Imagine a few of your favorites as you retreat for a moment today. Then consider: Is there a word that could have the same effect on your soul?

Much like the sounds of nature, the right phrases spoken just when we most need to hear them have an amazing capacity to soothe and restore. "I love you," "I'll be there," and "I'll help" are just a few. Yet one word you might not think of until you really need to hear it is the word *forgiven*. This one rarely used word holds the power of restoration like no other word on earth, for it can restore not only a heart or mind, but a relationship as well.

Consider the last time your child disobeyed your instruction or behaved toward you in an unloving way. Do you remember how much your child needed to receive your forgiveness? You could probably see the relief on her face and feel the release in her body as you accepted her back into your arms, forgiven and restored.

There is now no condemnation for those who are in Christ Jesus.

—Romans 8:1

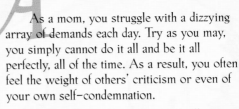

A Moment to Reflect

As a mom, you struggle with a dizzying array of demands each day. Try as you may, you simply cannot do it all and be it all perfectly, all of the time. As a result, you often feel the weight of others' criticism or even of your own self-condemnation.

Did you know that today God offers a relationship in which you are not condemned? Whether you have failed in some area or whether you are simply feeling the weight of others' expectations, turn to God in prayer. Experience relief and release as he accepts you into his arms, forgiven and restored.

When condemnation speaks to me, and I feel bound,
When those I love most seem to feel I've let them down,
When my soul aches
And my heart breaks
With heaviness and fear,
I run to You for my rescue, and Your arms draw me near.
Then You say, "Forgiven.
Child of Mine, find rest here.
You are forgiven."

—MELINDA MAHAND

25

If we confess our sins to God, he will keep his promise and do what is right: he will forgive us our sins and purify us from all our wrongdoing.

1 John 1:9 GNT

A Moment to Refresh

God did not send his Son into the world to condemn the world, but to save the world through him.

John 3:17

You are forgiving and good, O Lord, abounding in love to all who call to you. Hear my prayer, O LORD; listen to my cry for mercy. In the day of my trouble I will call to you, for you will answer me.

Psalm 86:5–7

By the blood of Christ we are set free, that is, our sins are forgiven. How great is the grace of God, which he gave to us in such large measure!

Ephesians 1:7–8 GNT

If the will of God was for you to be punished, then the heart of God would not have provided for your forgiveness.

❧

—MELINDA MAHAND

Blessed is he whose
transgressions are forgiven,
whose sins are covered.
Blessed is the man
whose sin the LORD does not count against
him and in whose spirit is no deceit.

Psalm 32:1–2

"I, even I, am he who blots out
your transgressions, for my own sake,
and remembers your sins no more,"
says the Lord.

Isaiah 43:25

I want you to know that through Jesus the
forgiveness of sins is proclaimed to you.
Through him everyone who believes is
justified from everything you could not be
justified from by the law of Moses.

Acts 13:38–39

In these days of guilt complexes, perhaps the most glorious word in the English language is "forgiven."

❧

—BILLY GRAHAM

Longing for Acceptance

A Moment to Pause   Retreat today to a place of quietness, a place where you can be still and become aware of God's presence with you. Welcome God into these moments and sense his love for you.

Although you may need to pause often in order to sense God's presence, you have no need to pause to sense the presence of other people. You perceive their presence instantly. Your awareness of their presence has a stronger impact than you may realize, for that presence speaks to one of your deepest human needs—the need to be accepted.

You spend much of your time trying to receive acceptance from those in your presence. That desire influences everything from the way you speak to the way you dress. Even moms are prone to fine-tune an image so that it will be received with acceptance. As an adult, you simply have become so polished at it that you are less obvious doing it than are your older children.

Once again, God offers to meet you at the place of your deepest need. As his children, you are truly accepted, not for how you look or how you behave, but simply for who you are.

Christianity is about acceptance,
and if God accepts me as I am,
then I had better do the same for others.
—Hugh Montefiore

A Moment to Reflect

Knowledge of God's acceptance can have a powerful impact on your prayer life. If you have struggled with feelings of inadequacy or inferiority that have kept you from the Father, understanding his acceptance frees you to go to him with confidence and thanksgiving today.

Yet God's acceptance has an impact not just on your life, but also on the lives of those around you. Since God accepts you, he desires that you accept others. Acceptance is an appealing quality to a person who has never experienced it. Acceptance opened many doors for Jesus to teach people about the Father. It will open many doors for you to teach about him as well.

Whether men be pleased or displeased, whether they judge you, or whatever they call you, it will seem a small matter to you in comparison to God's judgment. You live not on them. You can bear their displeasure, censures, and reproaches, if God be but pleased.

—RICHARD BAXTER

Accept one another...just as Christ accepted
you, in order to bring praise to God.

Romans 15:7

A Moment to Refresh

I now realize how true it is that God does not
show favoritism but accepts men from every
nation who fear him and do what is right.

Acts 10:34–35

This is love: not that we loved God, but that he
loved us and sent his Son as an atoning
sacrifice for our sins. Dear friends, since God
so loved us, we also ought to love one another.

1 John 4:10–11

The LORD takes delight in his people;
he crowns the humble with salvation.
Let the saints rejoice in this honor
and sing for joy on their beds.
May the praise of God be in their mouths.

Psalm 149:4–6

We can do nothing if we hate ourselves, or feel that all our actions are doomed to failure because of our own worthlessness. We have to take ourselves, good and bad alike, on trust before we can do anything.

—MARTIN ISRAEL

Let the words of my mouth, and the meditation of my heart, be acceptable in thy sight, O LORD, my strength, and my redeemer.

Psalm 19:14 KJV

Offer yourselves as a living sacrifice to God, dedicated to his service and pleasing to him. This is true worship that you should offer. Do not conform yourselves to the standards of this world, but let God transform you inwardly by a complete change of your mind. Then you will be able to know the will of God—what is good and is pleasing to him and is perfect.

Romans 12:1–2 GNT

The LORD delights in those who fear him, who put their hope in his unfailing love.

Psalm 147:11

Accept the fact that you are accepted.

—PAUL TILLICH

Fearless Nights

A Moment to Pause

On this day, wait until evening to retreat alone for a while. Go outdoors and take in the peaceful elements that come with the dusk—the chorus of nighttime animals, the cool evening breeze, perhaps even a gentle twilight shower.

This setting that signals such peace and tranquility sometimes brings with it a multitude of worries and fears. Just as children sometimes do, moms also may lie anxious in bed. In the darkness of nighttime, your heart and mind seem especially susceptible to troubling voices that recount the unfinished tasks of the day, the litany of demands that tomorrow brings, the potential struggles or trials in your future, and the never-ending supply of what-if's.

Yet unlike your children, you do not feel the freedom to cry out in the night, to run to the side of someone who loves you and exclaim, "I'm afraid." Instead you toss and turn and add yet one more sleepless night to the tally.

In these restless moments, you feel alone and vulnerable. You may wonder, "Where is God in this darkness?"

We must welcome the night. It's the only time
that the stars shine.
—Michel Quoist

Darkness or light, nighttime or day—such variations do not alter God's presence. Yet they often alter your human thoughts and emotions. Whether in a time of literal darkness or of soul darkness, meditate on the verses on the following pages. Spend your time praying and meditating on the Lord. Keep a Bible beside your bed, for nothing has power to dispel fear and uncertainty like God's Word.

God is present, even in the darkness, and he will respond when we turn to him for comfort and help.

If you happen to fall asleep as you spend time with the Lord, there is no need to feel guilt. You have just found how to rest in the Father's arms.

Be thou my vision, O Lord of my heart;
naught be all else to me, save that thou art—
thou my best thought, by day or by night,
waking or sleeping, thy presence my light.

❧

—IRISH POEM, CA. 700,
VERSIFIED BY MARY ELIZABETH BYRNE,
TRANSLATED BY ELEANOR H. HULL

I will lie down and sleep in peace,
for you alone, O LORD,
make me dwell in safety.

Psalm 4:8

A Moment to Refresh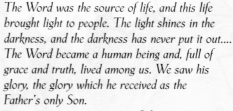

The Word was the source of life, and this life
brought light to people. The light shines in the
darkness, and the darkness has never put it out....
The Word became a human being and, full of
grace and truth, lived among us. We saw his
glory, the glory which he received as the
Father's only Son.

John 1:4–5, 14 GNT

By day the LORD directs his love,
at night his song is with me—
a prayer to the God of my life.

Psalm 42:8

This...is the message which we have heard of
him, and declare unto you, that God is light, and
in him is no darkness at all.

1 John 1:5 KJV

I would rather walk with God in the dark than go alone in the light.

—MARY GARDINER BRAINARD

Who among you fears the LORD
and obeys the word of his servant?
Let him who walks in the dark,
who has no light,
trust in the name of the LORD
and rely on his God.

Isaiah 50:10

If I say, "Surely the darkness will hide me
and the light become night around me,"
even the darkness will not be dark to you;
the night will shine like the day,
for darkness is as light to you.

Psalm 139:11–12

At night my soul longs for You,
Indeed, my spirit within me seeks You
diligently, O LORD.

Isaiah 26:9 NASB

Faith grows only in the dark. You've got to trust him when you can't trace him. That's faith.

—LYELL RADER

Ever Near

A Moment to Pause Enjoy a change of pace just now as you pause to spend a few minutes in quiet stillness. Even as you slip away for this precious time alone, recognize that God is ever near. Invite him to share these moments of rest and meditation.

Discovering time to be alone seems especially difficult for busy moms. The daily tasks of maintaining a home and raising a family compel you to spend far more time caring for the needs of others than you spend caring for your own. Often one of the first areas to suffer is time spent with the Lord. How can you find time for prayer when brushing your teeth without interruption is a rare treat?

Fortunately, God does not demand that you be alone or that you be otherwise unoccupied in order to talk with him. He is always present with you, ready to listen and to respond to you. Your challenge is to become consciously aware of his presence on a daily, moment-by-moment basis. He is with you as you drive the car, take a shower, or prepare dinner for your family. So rather than waiting until you are alone and unoccupied to speak to him, you can begin a conversation anytime and anywhere you choose.

God is always near you and with you;
leave Him not alone.
—Brother Lawrence

A Moment to Reflect

I Imagine calling a good friend on the phone and never hanging up. That kind of communication is available to you today, for God actually is a friend, always intimately near you, and he invites you to keep the lines of communication open during your daily activities. Perhaps this type of communication with the Lord is exactly what the apostle Paul had in mind when he said to "pray continually" (1 Thessalonians 5:17).

What are some times today when you can talk to God as you carry out your common tasks? Let conversation with him become comfortable and common, for you will receive instruction, protection, communion, provision—whatever the need of your soul—as you learn to recognize he is ever near.

When we sing, "Draw me nearer, nearer, blessed Lord," we are not thinking of the nearness of place, but of the nearness of relationship. It is for increasing degrees of awareness that we pray, for a more perfect consciousness of the divine Presence. We need never shout across the spaces to an absent God. He is nearer than our own soul, closer than our most secret thoughts.

⌇

—A. W. TOZER

In Christ Jesus you who once were far away
have been brought near through
the blood of Christ.

Ephesians 2:13

A Moment to Refresh

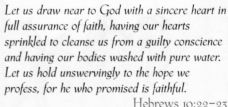

Let us draw near to God with a sincere heart in
full assurance of faith, having our hearts
sprinkled to cleanse us from a guilty conscience
and having our bodies washed with pure water.
Let us hold unswervingly to the hope we
profess, for he who promised is faithful.

Hebrews 10:22–23

The LORD is righteous in all his ways
and loving toward all he has made.
The LORD is near to all who call on him,
to all who call on him in truth.
He fulfills the desires of those who fear him;
he hears their cry and saves them.

Psalm 145:17–19

Let us...approach the throne of grace with
confidence, so that we may receive mercy and
find grace to help us in our time of need.

Hebrews 4:16

What our Lord did was done with this intent, and this alone, that he might be with us and we with him.

—MEISTER ECKHART

The LORD appeared to us
in the past, saying:
"I have loved you with an everlasting love;
I have drawn you with loving-kindness."
Jeremiah 31:3

The LORD is near to those who are
discouraged;
he saves those who have lost all hope.
Good people suffer many troubles,
but the LORD preserves them completely.
Psalm 34:18–19 GNT

God, who is everywhere, never leaves us.

—THOMAS MERTON

From one human being God created all
races of people and made them live
throughout the whole earth. He himself fixed
beforehand the exact times and the limits of
the places where they would live. He did this
so that they would look for him, and perhaps
find him as they felt around for him. Yet
God is actually not far from any one of us.
Acts 17:26–27 GNT

Worth the Wait

For a few moments today, step away from your fast-paced world. Find a place of stillness in your soul. Pause and rest there for a while, waiting for God to speak to your heart.

All of nature teaches us to wait. The dormant seed patiently awaits the return of spring. The songbird watches for each new dawn. Even the lowly caterpillar bides her time within a lonely chrysalis chamber until new wings form and signal the moment of her emergence. Some things are worth waiting for.

What events have been worth waiting for in your life? The return of a loved one who had been away? A special get-together with a good friend? The birth of your child? Regardless of which events come to mind, the aspect that made each wait worthwhile was not the event itself, but the intimate relationship that was inherent in the event. The loved one, the friend, the child was worth waiting for.

Likewise, God asks us to wait for him, not because he wants to inconvenience us or frustrate us, but because he wants a relationship with us. By waiting on God, we demonstrate that we are willing to invest our time developing an intimate relationship with him.

*I will watch for the LORD; I will wait
confidently for God, who will save me. My God
will hear me.*
—Micah 7:7 GNT

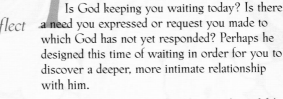

A Moment to Reflect

Is God keeping you waiting today? Is there a need you expressed or request you made to which God has not yet responded? Perhaps he designed this time of waiting in order for you to discover a deeper, more intimate relationship with him.

Often, it is as you wait that you learn life's deepest lessons regarding faith, prayer, and simple trust. If you are experiencing a period of waiting just now, determine to use this time to grow more steadfast in your faith and more consistent in your prayer. Then begin to live each day with hope and expectancy, for God does respond to those who wait.

I charge my thoughts, be humble still,
All my carriage mild,
Content, my Father, with Thy will,
And quiet as a child.
The patient soul, the lowly mind
Shall have a large reward:
Let saints in sorrow lie resigned,
And trust a faithful Lord.

—Isaac Watts

They that wait upon the LORD shall renew
their strength; they shall mount up with wings
as eagles; they shall run, and not be weary; and
they shall walk, and not faint.

Isaiah 40:31 KJV

A Moment to Refresh

I waited patiently for the LORD;
he turned to me and heard my cry.
He lifted me out of the slimy pit,
out of the mud and mire;
he set my feet on a rock
and gave me a firm place to stand.
He put a new song in my mouth,
a hymn of praise to our God.
Many will see and fear
and put their trust in the LORD.

Psalm 40:1-3

I am still confident of this:
I will see the goodness of the LORD
in the land of the living.
Wait for the LORD;
be strong and take heart
and wait for the LORD.

Psalm 27:13-14

There is no place for faith if we expect God to fulfill immediately what he promises.

—JOHN CALVIN

*Since ancient times no one has heard,
no ear has perceived,
no eye has seen any God besides you,
who acts on behalf of those who wait for him.*
Isaiah 64:4

*Hope that is seen is no hope at all. Who
hopes for what he already has? But if we
hope for what we do not yet have,
we wait for it patiently.*
Romans 8:24–25

*Out of the depths I cry to you, O LORD;
O Lord, hear my voice.
Let your ears be attentive
to my cry for mercy....
I wait for the LORD, my soul waits,
and in his word I put my hope.
My soul waits for the Lord
more than watchmen wait for the morning,
more than watchmen wait for the morning.*
Psalm 130:1–2, 5–6

*We must wait for
God, long, meekly,
in the wind and
wet, in the thunder
and lightning, in the
cold and the dark.
Wait, and he will
come. He never
comes to those who
do not wait.*

—FREDERICK
WILLIAM FABER

43

Hand in Hand

A Moment to Pause Allow yourself to lean back and reminisce about times you have held the hand of someone you love. Recall the deep feelings of acceptance and security that those moments offered. Remember the welcome realization that you were not alone on life's journey.

Although the gesture of taking someone's hand seems simple, it often can fulfill physical, emotional, and even spiritual needs. For when two people join hands, they join hearts as well.

One such moment took place when Lisa's son was two years old. A forested embankment behind their home led to a shallow, spring-fed creek. Although Lisa's son begged daily to splash his toes in the cool, crystal water, she dared not let him head down the bank alone. She knew his unsteady legs and the steep grade of the hill would result in his being hurled headlong down the bank and face first into the water.

So each day Lisa simply took her son by the hand and walked with him down the hill. Although stumbling was still a distinct possibility, she knew her son would not fall because his hand was securely clasped in hers. Lisa knew her child would be safe because he was not alone.

If the LORD delights in a man's way, he makes
his steps firm; though he stumble, he will not fall,
for the LORD upholds him with his hand.
—Psalm 37:23-24

44

A Moment to Reflect

Today the Lord is offering to take your hand and walk beside you on life's journey. He wants to be not only your companion, but your guide and protector as well. Although you may be hurt by an occasional stumble, you will not be destroyed by a headlong fall as long as you are walking hand in hand with him.

Choose to take God's hand and join your heart with his. Just as a toddling child becomes more and more sure of his steps as he holds a parent's hand, so your steps will become firm as you walk with the Lord. He will meet all your needs, and you will experience the incredible reality that you are not alone.

Hand in hand with one who loves me,
Hand in hand, I safely go
Through the valleys of life's journey,
Then on to new heights in my soul.
Hand in hand with one who loves me,
Hand in hand, I am secure
As my father ever gently
Guides my steps and makes them sure.

—MELINDA MAHAND

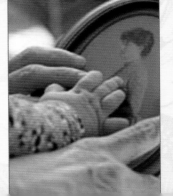

45

Jesus said, "I give [my followers] eternal life,
and they shall never perish; no one can snatch
them out of my hand. My Father, who has
given them to me, is greater than all; no one
can snatch them out of my Father's hand."

John 10:28–29

A Moment to Refresh

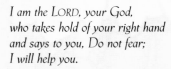

I am the LORD, your God,
who takes hold of your right hand
and says to you, Do not fear;
I will help you.

Isaiah 41:13

Thus saith God the LORD, he that created the
heavens, and stretched them out; he that spread
forth the earth, and that which cometh out of it;
he that giveth breath unto the people upon it,
and spirit to them that walk therein: I the LORD
have called thee in righteousness, and will hold
thine hand, and will keep thee.

Isaiah 42:5–6 KJV

To God who is able to keep you from falling
and to present you before his glorious presence
without fault and with great joy—to the only
God our Savior be glory, majesty, power and
authority, through Jesus Christ our Lord,
before all ages, now and forevermore!

Jude 24–25

*The hand of God is strong enough
to protect His feeblest child,
yet gentle enough to lead that same child homeward.*

—MELINDA MAHAND

*O LORD, you protect me and save me;
your care has made me great,
and your power has kept me safe.
You have kept me from being captured,
and I have never fallen.*

Psalm 18:35–36 GNT

*I was pushed back and about to fall,
but the LORD helped me.
The LORD is my strength and my song;
he has become my salvation.
Shouts of joy and victory
resound in the tents of the righteous:
"The LORD's right hand has done mighty
things! The LORD's right hand is lifted high;
the LORD 's right hand has done
mighty things!" I will not die but live,
and will proclaim what the LORD has done.*

Psalm 118:13–17

*Great eagles fly
alone; great lions
hunt alone; great
souls walk alone—
alone with God.*

—LEONARD
RAVENHILL

A Place for Hope

A Moment to Pause

For a few minutes today, plan to experience the simple pleasure of momentary rest. As you begin to relax, turn your thoughts to the things in life that bring you hope. What are your hopes for yourself today? What are your hopes for tomorrow?

Do you remember when you were a young child, innocent and passionate in your hopes for the future? You eagerly anticipated such modest events as taking a turn in a game or going to visit your grandparents. You regarded those simple delights with great expectation and confidence. You wholeheartedly threw yourself into hope with no thought of failure or disappointment.

Why do you suppose you unabashedly expressed hope? Perhaps because your loving family relationships had taught you it was safe to trust. Trust is, in fact, the foundation upon which hope is built. A person who has learned to trust is able to hope.

Somewhere between childhood and adulthood you may have lost your innocence and passion regarding hope. You may have experienced disappointments in your relationships. You may have learned that hope can be ill–founded or misplaced, and you may have ceased to trust. Ultimately, tragically, you might have even ceased to hope.

Never deprive someone of hope—
it may be all they have.
—Author Unknown

A Moment to Reflect

Today God offers a relationship in which you can place your confidence, a relationship in which you can place your trust. His joy is to fill your heart with great expectation and to teach you once again to innocently, passionately hope.

Consider again your hopes for this day and for tomorrow. You can trust God in each of those areas today. You can choose to wholeheartedly throw yourself into relationship with him. Ask him to recreate in your heart a place for hope. His love will not fail or disappoint you. His love will give you hope, be your hope, and satisfy your hope.

In Thee, O Lord God, I put all my hope and my refuge, on Thee I lay all my tribulation and anguish.... For many friends shall not profit, nor strong helpers be able to succor, nor prudent counselors to give a useful answer, nor the books of the learned to console, nor any precious substance to deliver, nor any secret and beautiful place to give shelter, if Thou Thyself do not assist, help, strengthen, comfort, instruct, keep in safety.

—THOMAS À KEMPIS

49

May the God of hope fill you with all joy and peace as you trust in him, so that you may overflow with hope by the power of the Holy Spirit.

Romans 15:13

A Moment to Refresh

Why are you downcast, O my soul? Why so disturbed within me? Put your hope in God, for I will yet praise him, my Savior and my God.

Psalm 43:5

Let us give thanks to the God and Father of our Lord Jesus Christ! Because of his great mercy he gave us new life by raising Jesus Christ from death. This fills us with a living hope, and so we look forward to possessing the rich blessings that God keeps for his people. He keeps them for you in heaven, where they cannot decay or spoil or fade away.

1 Peter 1:3–4 GNT

Everything that was written in the past was written to teach us, so that through endurance and the encouragement of the Scriptures we might have hope.

Romans 15:4

The future is as bright as the promises of God.

—ADONIRAM JUDSON

"I know the plans I have for you," declares the LORD, "plans to prosper you and not to harm you, plans to give you hope and a future."

Jeremiah 29:11

Faith is being sure of what we hope for and certain of what we do not see.

Hebrews 11:1

I will always have hope; I will praise you more and more. My mouth will tell of your righteousness, of your salvation all day long, though I know not its measure.

Psalm 71:14–15

Hope does not disappoint us, because God has poured out his love into our hearts by the Holy Spirit, whom he has given us.

Romans 5:5

We must accept finite disappointment, but we must never lose infinite hope.

—MARTIN LUTHER KING JR.

All Eyes on You

A Moment to Pause

Your eyes work hard, so offer them a soothing treat today by placing a cool cucumber slice or a damp tea bag over each lid. As you rest your eyes, meditate on the blessing of God's eyes watching over you.

Now consider the vast amount of information your eyes give you. Each day your eyes capture innumerable visual signals that tell you about the circumstances and people in your world. Your eyes help you determine whether your spouse is sick or well, hurried or relaxed. They help you discern whether a friend is contented or upset. They give you information to help you decide whether a particular situation is safe or dangerous. They tell you what your child is doing or even what he is thinking of doing. Your eyes help you evaluate situations, emotions, and behaviors in order to guide, encourage, strengthen, protect, and care for yourself and those around you.

Yet your eyes have limits. They cannot go everywhere your loved ones go. They grow weary and must rest. They have not seen every detail of the past, nor can they foresee any detail of the future. Human eyes are, after all, human eyes.

I will instruct you and teach you in the way which you should go; I will counsel you with My eye upon you.
—Psalm 32:8 NASB

A Moment to Reflect

The eyes of God have no human limits. They reach into every corner of this universe. They pierce the past and the future. They do not grow weary but are always awake, always watchful. Not even a sparrow can fall to the ground without God seeing, knowing, caring.

Recognize today that God watches for the same reasons you watch. God watches because God loves. His eyes are on you to guide, encourage, reprimand, protect, comfort, strengthen, and care for you. Thank him today for encompassing you with his eyes. Trust him to see and act on your behalf in every situation.

It is an infinite mistake to suppose that God is enthroned far beyond the stars, in any sense which separates him from immediate contact with ourselves. . . . This is the essential glory of God, and the mystery of his being, that he is far away, yet near at hand; near at hand, yet losing nothing through familiarity; far away, yet able to come at a moment's notice to guide, inspire, and sanctify his trustful children.

—JOSEPH PARKER

53

The eyes of the Lord are on the righteous and his ears are attentive to their prayer.

1 Peter 3:12

A Moment to Refresh

The eyes of the LORD range throughout the earth to strengthen those whose hearts are fully committed to him.

2 Chronicles 16:9

Where could I go to escape from you? Where could I get away from your presence? If I went up to heaven, you would be there; if I lay down in the world of the dead, you would be there. If I flew away beyond the east or lived in the farthest place in the west, you would be there to lead me, you would be there to help me.

Psalm 139:7–10 GNT

The eyes of the LORD are on those who fear him, on those whose hope is in his unfailing love.

Psalm 33:18

As a Christian is never out of the reach of God's hand,
so he is never out of the view of God's eye.

—Thomas Brooks

This is what the LORD says: "Heaven is my throne, and the earth is my footstool. Where is the house you will build for me? Where will my resting place be? Has not my hand made all these things, and so they came into being?" declares the LORD. "This is the one I esteem: he who is humble and contrite in spirit, and trembles at my word."

Isaiah 66:1–2

The eyes of the LORD are in every place, beholding the evil and the good.

Proverbs 15:3 KJV

Examine me, O LORD, and try me; test my mind and my heart. For Your lovingkindness is before my eyes, and I have walked in Your truth.

Psalm 26:2–3 NASB

I believe he sees;
therefore, even when
I don't see, I still
believe.

—Melinda Mahand

God Is Ready to Listen

A Moment to Pause   Slow down today to refresh your spirit with a few moments with God. Choose a comfy spot to sit outdoors, or recline on a sunlit sofa near a window in your home. Enjoy the beauty of God's world as you spend this brief time with him today.

Such moments are rare these days. In fact, we spend a great deal of our time and money making sure we can stay in constant touch with others who are important in our lives. We purchase everything from baby monitors to cell phones. We leave messages on answering machines and pagers. We master systems of overnight mail and e-mail. We sometimes resort to notes hastily scrawled with pen on paper.

Each of these communications devices attempts to bring together people who are separated by time, distance, or busy schedules. Yet even when we use them all and use them well, we are often left with the uneasy realization that our exchanges of information consist of shallow tidbits of facts or opinion rather than of true conversation.

There are no depths from which the prayer of faith cannot reach heaven.
—John Blanchard

A Moment to Reflect

Wherever you are today—whatever your need, whatever your heartache, whatever your fear—know that God is waiting to hear from you. You do not need high-tech communications systems to send your message to his ears. You can simply talk to him about the concerns that fill your heart. It truly is no more complicated than that. Just talk to him.

When you do, God will hear you. At the sound of your voice, he will listen patiently, attentively, and lovingly. Talk to God as you would confide in your best friend; enjoy the comfortable comraderie that comes from knowing that you are totally accepted as you are.

Never too far I've fled,
Never too softly said,
Never too choked with tears,
Never too wrapped in fears,
—My Father heard all.

Swift He ran to my side,
Heeded each anguished cry,
Brushed every tear away,
Strengthened me for the day,
—Answered my call.

—MELINDA MAHAND

The righteous cry out, and the LORD hears them; he delivers them from all their troubles.

Psalm 34:17

A Moment to Refresh

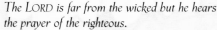

The LORD is far from the wicked but he hears the prayer of the righteous.

Proverbs 15:29

Jesus said, whatever you ask for in prayer, believe that you have received it, and it will be yours.

Mark 11:24

Before they call, I will answer; while they are still speaking I will hear.

Isaiah 65:24

Confess your sins to each other and pray for each other so that you may be healed. The prayer of a righteous man is powerful and effective. Elijah was a man just like us. He prayed earnestly that it would not rain, and it did not rain on the land for three and a half years. Again he prayed, and the heavens gave rain, and the earth produced its crops.

James 5:16–18

More things are wrought by prayer than this world dreams of.

—ALFRED, LORD TENNYSON

In my distress I called to the LORD; I cried to my God for help. From his temple he heard my voice; my cry came before him, into his ears.... He rescued me from my powerful enemy, from my foes, who were too strong for me.

Psalm 18:6, 17

My salvation and my honor depend on God; he is my mighty rock, my refuge. Trust in him at all times, O people; pour out your hearts to him, for God is our refuge.

Psalm 62:7–8

In Jesus and through faith in him we may approach God with freedom and confidence.... For this reason I kneel before the Father.

Ephesians 3:12, 14

Groanings which cannot be uttered are often prayers which cannot be refused.

—C. H. SPURGEON

Don't Wait Till Heaven

A Moment to Pause   Enjoy your soul retreat today in a comfortable place outdoors. Stretch out and spend a few moments gazing into the sky, whether daytime or nighttime. Consider eternity with God. What do you think heaven will be like? What do you look forward to about being there?

Heaven is assuredly a wonderful place, full of God's goodness and full of God's blessings. You do not have to wait till heaven to experience God's goodness and blessing. God desires for you to experience them right now, in this present life.

Sometimes, however, our vision blurs because we are focused on life's troubles and can't recognize God's goodness and blessing. Instead we may be like the child who chases his ball into the street. The child sees only his ball and not the approaching car. When his mother grabs him out of the street, the child recognizes only that his precious toy has been lost, and not that his life was not. Because he is focused on mourning his loss, he cannot appreciate being secure in the goodness and blessing of his mother's loving hand.

The LORD God is a sun and shield; the LORD
bestows favor and honor; no good thing does he
withhold from those whose walk is blameless.
—Psalm 84:11

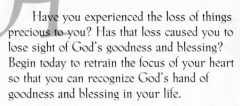

A Moment to Reflect

Have you experienced the loss of things precious to you? Has that loss caused you to lose sight of God's goodness and blessing? Begin today to retrain the focus of your heart so that you can recognize God's hand of goodness and blessing in your life.

What good thing has the Lord recently sent your way? What new opportunity has he given? In what area has he blessed you with a second chance? Who has he worked through to bring you help or encouragement? Recognize these gifts as being from the hand of God. Thank him for them individually and specifically. Then begin to watch for his goodness and blessing each day—because you really don't have to wait till heaven.

God often takes a course for accomplishing His purposes directly contrary to what our narrow views would prescribe. He brings a death upon our feelings, wishes, and prospects when He is about to give us the desire of our hearts.

—JOHN NEWTON

*Let them give thanks to the LORD for his
unfailing love and his wonderful deeds for men,
for he satisfies the thirsty and fills the hungry
with good things.*

Psalm 107:8–9

A Moment to Refresh

*Jesus said, "Is there anyone among you who, if
your child asks for bread, will give a stone? Or
if the child asks for a fish, will give a snake? If
you then, who are evil, know how to give good
gifts to your children, how much more will your
Father in heaven give good things to those who
ask him!"*

Matthew 7:9–11 NRSV

*The LORD upholds all those who fall and lifts
up all who are bowed down. The eyes of all
look to you, and you give them their food at the
proper time. You open your hand and satisfy the
desires of every living thing. The LORD is
righteous in all his ways and loving toward all
he has made.*

Psalm 145:14–17

Those blessings are sweetest that are won with prayer and worn with thanks.

—THOMAS GOODWIN

God is able to make all grace abound to you, so that in all things at all times, having all that you need, you will abound in every good work. As it is written: "He has scattered abroad his gifts to the poor; his righteousness endures forever."

2 Corinthians 9:8–9

Paul, Silas, and Timothy wrote: We constantly pray for you, that our God may count you worthy of his calling, and that by his power he may fulfill every good purpose of yours and every act prompted by your faith.

2 Thessalonians 1:11

Take delight in the LORD, and he will give you the desires of your heart. Commit your way to the LORD; trust in him, and he will act.

Psalm 37:4–5 NRSV

What kind of God are You, who does not make my dreams come true, but does things more impossible than even I can dream?

—MELINDA MAHAND

God's Awesome Answers

A Moment to Pause

Perhaps you need a change of pace today, a time to slow down, gather your thoughts, and refresh your soul. Take a break now to rest your body and quiet your mind for a few moments. Consider how amazing God's plan for your physical and mental being is. He created you in such a way that something as simple as rest can answer the needs of both soma and soul, bringing restoration and renewal.

Yet not every need is answered quite so simply. Sometimes your needs can loom like a mountain before you. They require answers that are awesome. They require might that is miraculous. They require nothing less than action from an all-powerful God.

As a mother, however, you have become used to being the one who answers questions and meets requests within your family. You are often the last person to express your needs or to ask for assistance. As a result, you are likely to be slow in turning to God for answers for yourself.

Today, be reminded that God is available to listen to your requests. He truly wants to hear them, and he truly promises to answer them, not with comforting platitudes but with awesome deeds.

You answer us with awesome deeds of righteousness, O God our Savior, the hope of all the ends of the earth and of the farthest seas.
—Psalm 65:5

A Moment to Reflect

What are your needs this moment? Do you face a situation that seems insurmountable? Do you need an answer that is awesome? If so, have you told God about it?

Go to God in prayer right now. Tell him about the needs, large or small, in your life. Nothing that concerns your heart is insignificant to him. Ask him to act on your behalf. Give your burdens to God; release your worries, your fears. When you do, he has promised to deliver tangible help and to work in wondrous ways. He is strong and able.

I got up early one morning
And rushed right into the day;
I had so much to accomplish
That I didn't have time to pray.
Problems just tumbled about me,
And heavier came each task;
"Why doesn't God help me?" I wondered.
He answered, "You didn't ask."

I woke up early this morning,
And paused before entering the day;
I had so much to accomplish
That I had to take time to pray.

—AUTHOR UNKNOWN

65

*They will tell of the power of your awesome
works, and I will proclaim your great deeds.
They will celebrate your abundant goodness
and joyfully sing of your righteousness.*

Psalm 145:6–7

A Moment to Refresh

*The Lord said, "Will not God bring about
justice for his chosen ones, who cry out to him
day and night? Will he keep putting them off? I
tell you, he will see that they get justice,
and quickly."*

Luke 18:7–8

*Then they cried to the LORD in their trouble,
and he saved them from their distress. He
brought them out of darkness and the deepest
gloom and broke away their chains. Let them
give thanks to the LORD for his unfailing love
and his wonderful deeds for men.*

Psalm 107:13–15

*Blessed is the man who always fears the Lord,
but he who hardens his heart falls into
trouble.... A faithful man will be richly blessed,
but one eager to get rich will not go unpunished.*

Proverbs 28:14, 20

We should believe nothing is too small to be named before God. What should we think of the patient who told his doctor he was ill, but never went into particulars?

—JOHN CHARLES RYLE

When I was in trouble, I called to the LORD, and he answered me.

Psalm 120:1 GNT

"Have faith in God," Jesus answered. "I tell you the truth, if anyone says to this mountain, 'Go, throw yourself into the sea,' and does not doubt in his heart but believes that what he says will happen, it will be done for him."

Mark 11:22–23

When you pray, go into your room, close the door and pray to your Father, who is unseen. Then your Father, who sees what is done in secret, will reward you.

Matthew 6:6

A prayer warrior is a person who is convinced that God is omnipotent— that God has the power to do anything, to change anyone, and to intervene in any circumstance. A person who truly believes this refuses to doubt God.

—AUTHOR UNKNOWN

Angels at Your Side

A Moment to Pause

Withdraw somewhere alone. Lean back and let the burdens and the tensions of the day drift away as you indulge in a time of peaceful relaxation. As you rest, look slowly to your left and to your right. Did you notice angels at your side? Probably not. Having angels at your side is not unusual—but being aware of them is.

Consider for a moment how the word *angel* is commonly used in day-to-day life. Especially helpful friends are sometimes called "angels." Sleeping children are sometimes called "angels." Even loved ones in heaven may sometimes be called "angels."

Yet the Bible teaches that angels are, in reality, none of these things. Angels are beings created by God to worship him, to serve as his messengers, and to carry out his purposes on earth. Angels, in fact, are especially active in the lives of God's people. Scripture describes them feeding Elijah in the wilderness, ministering to Christ after his temptation, delivering messages to God's children, and actively protecting them.

*Beside each believer stands an angel as protector
and shepherd leading him to life.*
—Basil the Great

A Moment to Reflect

The next time you wonder whether you are really important to God, remember that of all the tasks his angels could perform, God sends them to take care of you. Just as the President of the United States has his Secret Service agents, just as famous or wealthy people have their bodyguards, so God has placed angels by your side to guide and protect you.

This truth is a powerful statement of your importance in God's eyes! You are precious to him. You are valuable to him. You are loved by him.

Everlasting God, you have ordained and constituted in a wonderful order the ministries of angels and mortals: Mercifully grant that, as your holy angels always serve and worship you in heaven, so by your appointment they may help and defend us here on earth; through Jesus Christ our Lord, who lives and reigns with you and the Holy Spirit, one God, for ever and ever. Amen.

—*The Book of Common Prayer*

The angel of the LORD encamps around those who fear him, and he delivers them. Taste and see that the LORD is good; blessed is the man who takes refuge in him.

Psalm 34:7–8

A Moment to Refresh

Are not all angels ministering spirits sent to serve those who will inherit salvation?

Hebrews 1:14

The Lord will command his angels concerning you to guard you in all your ways.

Psalm 91:11

At the first light of dawn, the king got up and hurried to the lions' den. When he came near the den, he called to Daniel in an anguished voice, "Daniel, servant of the living God, has your God, whom you serve continually, been able to rescue you from the lions?" Daniel answered, "O king, live forever! My God sent his angel, and he shut the mouths of the lions. They have not hurt me, because I was found innocent in his sight."

Daniel 6:19–22

Sweet souls around us watch us still,
Press nearer to our side;
Into our thoughts, into our prayers,
With gentle helpings glide.

—HARRIET BEECHER STOWE

Do not forget to entertain strangers, for by so doing some people have entertained angels without knowing it.

Hebrews 13:2

At that time the sign of the Son of Man will appear in the sky, and all the nations of the earth will mourn. They will see the Son of Man coming on the clouds of the sky, with power and great glory. And he will send his angels with a loud trumpet call, and they will gather his elect from the four winds, from one end of the heavens to the other.

Matthew 24:30–31

God said to the Israelites, "I will send an angel ahead of you along the way and to bring you to the place I have prepared."

Exodus 23:20

The servants of Christ are protected by invisible, rather than visible, beings. But if these guard you, they do so because they have been summoned by your prayers.

—AMBROSE

Hold On

A Moment to Pause
Your hands work hard to hold many things. Treat them to luxury today. Squeeze lotion into a microwave–safe cup. Liquefy the lotion by heating it for five seconds in the microwave on full power. Test the temperature with your fingertip before slathering the lotion onto your hands. Let the lotion set on your hands for a few moments before rubbing it in. Feel the warmth penetrate your muscles, and enjoy the silky result.

As you enjoy this personal pampering, think of all the items your hands have held today. You held them because you felt a need for each one. Some you needed because they are useful or helpful. Others you needed because they are comforting or encouraging. Still others you needed simply because they are precious to your heart.

Now consider God's desire that you cling to or hold on to him. What does that desire communicate? God wants you to cling to him because he desires to help you, comfort you, encourage you, and be precious to your heart. While you cannot literally hold God in your hands, you can hold him in your thoughts, in your affections, and in your priorities.

To hold on to God is to rely on the fact that God
is there for me, and to live in this certainty.
—Karl Barth

72

A Moment to Reflect

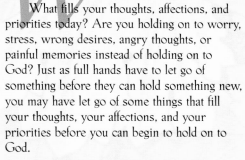

What fills your thoughts, affections, and priorities today? Are you holding on to worry, stress, wrong desires, angry thoughts, or painful memories instead of holding on to God? Just as full hands have to let go of something before they can hold something new, you may have let go of some things that fill your thoughts, your affections, and your priorities before you can begin to hold on to God.

Cling to God by spending time talking to him, reading his word, meditating on his word, or singing about his truths throughout your day. When worry, anger, wrong desires, or painful memories try to reclaim their old territory, refuse to accept them and instead hold fast to God.

Abide in me says Jesus. Cling to me. Stick fast to me. Live the life of close and intimate communion with me. Get nearer to me. . . . Never let go your hold on me for a moment. Be, as it were, rooted and planted in me. Do this and I will never fail you. I will ever abide in you.

—J. C. RYLE

Because you are my help, I sing in the shadow of your wings. My soul clings to you; your right hand upholds me.

Psalm 63:7–8

A Moment to Refresh

Jesus said, "Remain in me, and I will remain in you. No branch can bear fruit by itself; it must remain in the vine. Neither can you bear fruit unless you remain in me. I am the vine; you are the branches. If a man remains in me and I in him, he will bear much fruit; apart from me you can do nothing."

John 15:4–5

I will praise the LORD, who counsels me; even at night my heart instructs me. I have set the LORD always before me. Because he is at my right hand, I will not be shaken.

Psalm 16:7–8

Continue in him, so that when he appears we may be confident and unashamed before him at his coming.

1 John 2:28

Scripture and prayer serve as handles for those who would cling to God.

❧

—MELINDA MAHAND

Test everything. Hold on to the good. Avoid every kind of evil. May God himself, the God of peace, sanctify you through and through. May your whole spirit, soul and body be kept blameless at the coming of our Lord Jesus Christ. The one who calls you is faithful and he will do it.

1 Thessalonians 5:21–24

Jesus said, "As the Father has loved me, so I loved you. Now remain in my love.... I have told you this so that my joy may be in you that your joy may be complete."

John 15:9, 11

Let us press on to know the LORD. His going forth is as certain as the dawn; and He will come to us like the rain, like the spring rain watering the earth.

Hosea 6:3 NASB

He who clings to any creature must of necessity fail as the creature fails. But he who cleaves abidingly to Jesus shall be made firm in Him forever.

❧

—THOMAS À KEMPIS

Choosing to Trust

A Moment to Pause Settle into a favorite reading spot and prepare to enjoy some time with God. Invite God to speak to your heart. Recall the beginning of your relationship with him, and remember the simple trust you placed in his word and in his person.

Trust is a routine element of life. When you eat food at a restaurant, you trust that it is fresh. When you slow down on the highway, you trust that the brakes on your car work. Trust in "things" such as these comes easily and unconsciously.

Yet trust does not come so easily or unconsciously in relationships with people. Remember the last time you had a checkup with a new doctor? You made a conscious decision to let the doctor do the exam, a conscious decision that was probably rather difficult because you had no prior history in the relationship to prove the doctor's trustworthiness.

Amazingly, we sometimes treat God as we treat a new doctor. We find the choice to trust him a difficult one, even though he has proved his trustworthiness throughout generations since the beginning of time.

Trusting God does not mean you are sure of your destiny, only that you are sure of your company.
—*Melinda Mahand*

A Moment to Reflect God invites you to return to that relationship path you started down when first you trusted in him. He longs for you to look to him and his word for guidance and help on a daily basis.

Take out a pen and piece of paper. On one side of the paper, list times in your personal past when God proved his trustworthiness to you. On the other side, list situations you now face where you need to trust God. Talk to God about each situation. Make the conscious choice to trust him in that area. Let him prove himself to you once more.

Trust yourself and you are doomed to disappointment.

Trust in your friends and they will die and leave you.

Trust your money and you may have it taken away from you.

Trust in reputation and some slanderous tongues will blast it.

But trust in God and you are never to be confounded in time or in eternity.

—DWIGHT MOODY

The LORD is good, a refuge in time of trouble.
He cares for those who trust in him.

Nahum 1:6

A Moment to Refresh

Don't put your trust in human leaders; no
human being can save you. When they die, they
return to the dust; on that day all their plans
come to an end. Happy are those who have the
God of Jacob to help them and who depend on
the LORD their God, the Creator of heaven,
earth, and sea, and all that is in them. He
always keeps his promises.

Psalm 146:3–6 GNT

Trust in the LORD with all your heart; and lean
not on your own understanding; in all your
ways acknowledge him, and he will make your
paths straight.

Proverbs 3:5–6

Fear of man will prove to be a snare, but
whoever trusts in the LORD is kept safe.

Proverbs 29:25

*Trust the past to God's mercy, the present to God's love,
and the future to God's providence.*

࿓

—AUGUSTINE OF HIPPO

O LORD Almighty, blessed is the man who
trusts in you.

Psalm 84:12

Blessed is the man who trusts in the LORD,
whose confidence is in him. He will be like
a tree planted by the water that sends out
its roots by the stream. It does not fear
when heat comes; its leaves are always
green. It has no worries in a year of
drought and never fails to bear fruit.

Jeremiah 17:7–8

You will keep in perfect peace him whose
mind is steadfast, because he trusts in you.
Trust in the LORD forever, for the LORD,
the LORD, is the Rock eternal.

Isaiah 26:3–4

*The world instructs
us to try our very
best, but the Lord
instructs us to
simply trust his.*

࿓

—MELINDA MAHAND

79

A Place to Lean

A Moment to Pause

Take an opportunity simply to rest. Recline into the comfort of a cushiony sofa. As you lean back and relax, let tension melt from your muscles. Can you imagine your body resting this way if you did not have the cushions to lean against, the sofa to hold the weight of your body? Can you imagine your soul finding rest if there was no place to lean, no place to help bear the burdens that you carry in your heart and mind each day?

Your soul needs a place of rest just as your body does. Loved ones may sometimes be able to help. They may lend a hand or lend an ear and lighten your load. Even with support from loved ones in your life, some burdens remain yours alone. And God's.

This truth is clearly illustrated in a letter that Paul wrote. He told God's people to "help carry one another's burden" (GNT), and then he followed that advice with a gentle reminder that "each of you have to carry your own load." Some burdens remain on your shoulders regardless of the attentive people in your life, and those burdens are ones only God can bear.

God is not a deceiver, that he should offer to
support us, and then, when we lean upon Him,
should slip away from us.
—Augustine of Hippo

A Moment to Reflect

What burdens are weighing heavily on you? Read the following Bible verses and hear God's plea that you give those burdens to him. Notice he does not offer to "help" you with the burdens; he offers to completely bear them for you. He asks you to let go of them and cast them on him.

When you place your weight—the burden of your body—on the sofa, you know that it isn't going to collapse under you and let you fall.

Just as you trust the sofa on which you recline, so also trust God in whom you place the weight of your soul's burdens. Tell him about each one and make the conscious choice to leave the matter in his hands. Lean on him.

What a fellowship, what a joy divine,
Leaning on the everlasting arms;
What a blessedness, what a peace is mine,
Leaning on the everlasting arms.

—Elisha A. Hoffman

*Cast your cares on the LORD and he will
sustain you; he will never let the righteous fall.*
Psalm 55:22

A Moment to Refresh

*Cast all your anxiety on him because he cares
for you.... And the God of all grace, who called
you to his eternal glory in Christ, after you
have suffered a little while, will himself restore
you and make you strong, firm and steadfast.*
1 Peter 5:7, 10

*This is what the LORD says, "Stand at the
crossroads and look; ask for the ancient paths,
ask where the good way is, and walk in it, and
you will find rest for your souls."*
Jeremiah 6:16

*Jesus said, "Come to me, all you who are weary
and burdened, and I will give you rest. Take my
yoke upon you and learn from me, for I am
gentle and humble in heart, and you will find
rest for your souls."*
Matthew 11:28–29

*Everything a man leans upon but God, will be a dart
that will certainly pierce his heart through and
through. He, who leans only upon Christ, lives the
highest, choicest, safest, and sweetest life.*

— THOMAS BROOKS

*For thus said the Lord GOD, the Holy One
of Israel: In returning and rest you shall be
saved; in quietness and in trust shall be
your strength.*

Isaiah 30:15 NRSV

*King David praised the LORD. He said,
"LORD God of our ancestor Jacob, may
you be praised forever and ever! You are
great and powerful, glorious, splendid, and
majestic. Everything in heaven and earth is
yours, and you are king, supreme ruler
over all. All riches and wealth come from
you; you rule everything by your strength
and power; and you are able to make
anyone great and strong."*

1 Chronicles 29:10–12 GNT

*Jesus knows we
must come apart
and rest awhile, or
else we may just
plain come apart.*

— VANCE HAVNER

Handmade

A Moment to Pause

Sit in a comfortable spot outdoors or by a window through which you can view the beauty of God's creation. Isn't it amazing that every leaf unfolding, every cloud passing by, every insect buzzing—every created thing—is custom designed by God? Even more incredible, Scripture teaches that you are not only custom designed by God, but you are also handmade by God. Think of all that truth implies.

What do you enjoy creating? Do you paint, cook, landscape, or play an instrument? Do you decorate, sing, or sew? Do you write, enjoy crafts, or refinish furniture? Whatever your creative outlet, consider the extent to which the work of your hands is a work of self-expression and of love. To that same extent and more, you are the work of God's hands and as such are an expression of him and of his love.

Recognize that you, as God's workmanship, have high value. Begin today to discover his purposes for you, for by fulfilling his purposes you have the potential to affect not only life on earth, but life in eternity as well.

We are the handiwork of God.
—A. W. Tozer

A Moment to Reflect

You may tend to look in the mirror and find flaws. You may look at the abilities of others and feel that you were left out. Recognize today that God planned, designed, and made you by his own hand.

Thank God today for his glorious creation of you. God created you thoughtfully and purposefully; God does not make mistakes. Consider how to honor and care for you, his creation. Consider also how to fulfill the purposes he has for you, his creation.

The next time you look into the mirror
and feel inadequate or inferior. . .
The next time you face a God-given
opportunity to minister
in people's lives and feel challenged or scared. . .
The next time you long with all your heart to bring joy
to God yet feel like you couldn't possibly do so. . .
Just envision a label sewn onto your heart that reads:
"Handmade with Love by God."

—MELINDA MAHAND

85

We are God's workmanship, created in Christ
Jesus to do good works, which God prepared
in advance for us to do.

Ephesians 2:10

A Moment to Refresh

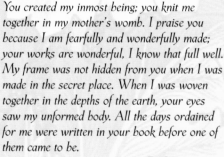

*You created my inmost being; you knit me
together in my mother's womb. I praise you
because I am fearfully and wonderfully made;
your works are wonderful, I know that full well.
My frame was not hidden from you when I was
made in the secret place. When I was woven
together in the depths of the earth, your eyes
saw my unformed body. All the days ordained
for me were written in your book before one of
them came to be.*

Psalm 139:13–16

*What are human beings that you are mindful of
them, mortals that you care for them? Yet you
have made them a little lower than God, and
crowned them with glory and honor. You have
given them dominion over the works of your
hands; you have put all things under their feet.*

Psalm 8:4–6 NRSV

My body was made for the love of God. Every cell in my body is a hymn to my creator and a declaration of love.

ॐ

—ERNESTO CARDENAL

Your hands made me and formed me; give me understanding to learn your commands.
Psalm 119:73

You are worthy, our Lord and God, to receive glory and honor and power, for you created all things, and by your will they were created and have their being.
Revelation 4:11

All you have made will praise you, O LORD; your saints will extol you. They will tell of the glory of your kingdom and speak of your might, so that all men may know of your mighty acts and the glorious splendor of your kingdom.
Psalm 145:10–12

God does not love us because we are valuable. We are valuable because God loves us.

ॐ

—FULTON JOHN SHEEN

Power You Can Rely On

A Moment to Pause

Is the sun shining today? If it is, go outdoors for a few moments of quiet meditation and think of all that our nearest star provides to the earth—energy for plants to make food, Vitamin D for our bodies, light and warmth for all living creatures. Yes, the sun is one of God's many blessings to his creation, but it is also a spectacular illustration of his power.

Consider that the sun is large enough to contain 1.3 million Earths. At its center, temperatures reach as high as 27 million degrees Fahrenheit. The rays emitted by the sun travel 93 million miles to earth in only eight minutes. Although we depend upon these rays for warmth, light, food, and energy, we cannot look directly upon their brilliant and powerful source.

As incredible as this heavenly body seems to us, the power of the sun is infinitesimal compared to the infinite power of God. For our sun is neither the biggest nor the brightest star in the galaxy, and it—as well as untold billions of other stars—was called into existence by a mere word from the Lord. Such power is incomprehensible to us, and yet this very power is accessible to us as children of God.

You will never need more than God can supply.
—J. I. Packer

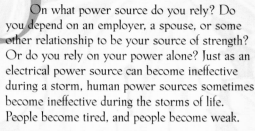

A Moment to Reflect

On what power source do you rely? Do you depend on an employer, a spouse, or some other relationship to be your source of strength? Or do you rely on your power alone? Just as an electrical power source can become ineffective during a storm, human power sources sometimes become ineffective during the storms of life. People become tired, and people become weak.

Today God offers to be a power source on whom you can rely. Since God is powerful enough to call the mighty sun into existence, surely he is capable of handling the details of your life. Tell him just now about situations that have recently overwhelmed you. Give him the opportunity to work powerfully on your behalf today.

I sing the mighty power of God,
That made the mountains rise;
That spread the flowing seas abroad,
And built the lofty skies.

There's not a plant or flower below,
But makes Thy glories known;
And clouds arise, and tempests blow,
By order from Thy throne.

While all that borrows life from Thee
Is ever in Thy care,
And everywhere that man can be,
Thou, God, art present there.

—Isaac Watts

89

No one is like you, O LORD; you are great,
and your name is mighty in power.

Jeremiah 10:6

A Moment to Refresh

I can do everything through him who gives me
strength.

Philippians 4:13

Great is our LORD and mighty in power; his
understanding has no limit. The LORD sustains
the humble but casts the wicked to the ground.
Sing to the LORD with thanksgiving; make
music to our God on the harp. He covers the
sky with clouds; he supplies the earth with rain
and makes grass grow on the hills. He provides
food for the cattle and for the young ravens
when they call.

Psalm 147:5–9

"Not by might nor by power, but by my Spirit,"
says the LORD Almighty.

Zechariah 4:6

When a man has no strength, if he leans on God, he becomes powerful.

—Dwight L. Moody

God made the earth by his power; he founded the world by his wisdom and stretched out the heavens by his understanding. When he thunders, the waters in the heavens roar; he makes clouds rise from the ends of the earth. He sends lightning with the rain and brings out the wind from his storehouses.

Jeremiah 10:12–13

Yours, O LORD, is the greatness and the power and the glory and the majesty and the splendor, for everything in heaven and earth is yours. Yours, O LORD, is the kingdom; you are exalted as head over all.

1 Chronicles 29:11

The same power that brought Christ back from the dead is operative within those who are Christ's.

—Leon Lamb Morris

Letting Go of Worry

A Moment to Pause

How has today been so far? Give yourself a few minutes to lean back and take several long, slow, deep breaths. As you exhale, feel the tension lift from your shoulders and allow the worries of the day to leave your mind.

Kim is a middle-aged mom who sometimes discovers a new worry her heart needs to let go of. During these times, she thinks of when her daughter was a baby. At six months old, Jenna began drinking from a bottle. So each night Kim would prepare a bottle for Jenna's early morning feeding and place it in the refrigerator. Then when a hungry cry rang out in the wee morning hours, all Kim had to do was heat the bottle.

Kim's heart would have broken if she had thought that Jenna spent one moment of the night worrying about whether there would be any milk for her the next morning. Kim would also have been hurt if she had thought that Jenna spent her nights plotting foolish and unnecessary schemes to get her needs met. As a young mother, Kim had known what Jenna's needs were and had been prepared to fulfill them. Kim had been ready to respond at the sound of her baby's cry.

Jenna had no reason to worry, no reason to fear. She could rest securely in the assurance that her needs would be filled. All she had to do was ask.

Worry has an active imagination.
—*D. Martin Lloyd-Jones*

A Moment to Reflect

God knows you as intimately as a parent knows a child. Your needs do not surprise or intimidate him any more than a baby's need for milk surprises or intimidates a mother. God knows every one of your needs and is prepared to fulfill them before you even ask. Anxious days and sleepless nights are unnecessary—and what is more, they break your heavenly Father's heart.

Talk to God about the things that concern you this day, and seek His provision. Meet God in prayer and find your every need fulfilled.

When your worries seem to be many,
and your friends seem to be few,
When you're looking for something that's faithful,
When you're looking for someone who's true,
In the stillness of the nighttime or the pressing of the day,
Turn your anxious thoughts toward the heavens,
And impel your heart to pray.
For your God is always nearby;
He will come at the sound of your cry.

—MELINDA MAHAND

I said, "I am falling"; but your constant love,
O LORD, held me up. Whenever I am
anxious and worried, you comfort me and
make me glad.

Psalm 94:18–19 GNT

A Moment to Refresh

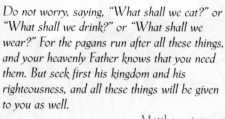

Do not worry, saying, "What shall we eat?" or
"What shall we drink?" or "What shall we
wear?" For the pagans run after all these things,
and your heavenly Father knows that you need
them. But seek first his kingdom and his
righteousness, and all these things will be given
to you as well.

Matthew 6:31–33

Do not be anxious about anything, but in
everything, by prayer and petition, with
thanksgiving, present your requests to God.
And the peace of God, which transcends all
understanding, will guard your hearts and your
minds in Christ Jesus.

Philippians 4:6–7

Worry never enhances your tomorrows. It only wastes your todays.

✄

—MELINDA MAHAND

Listen to my cry for help, my King and my God, for to you I pray. In the morning, O LORD, you hear my voice; in the morning I lay my requests before you and wait in expectation.

Psalm 5:2–3

Who by worrying can add a single hour to his life? Since you cannot do this very little thing, why do you worry about the rest?

Luke 12:25–26

Be at rest once more, O my soul, for the LORD has been good to you.

Psalm 116:7

Worry is like a rocking chair. It will give you something to do, but it won't get you anywhere.

✄

—AUTHOR UNKNOWN

Possibilities

A Moment to Pause

Do you remember when playgrounds were places of marvel, filled with the crystal laughter of other children in their merriment? Can you recall digging gleefully in a sandbox, hoping to discover a wonderful treasure? Does the memory return of a swing that seemed to sprout wings and take you soaring above the clouds? As children, playgrounds offered us a world of fascination where anything seemed possible. Yet the adult world called us to leave the playground, and increasingly life began to reveal many seeming impossibilities. Today's good news, however, is that God does not recognize anything as impossible, for he is a God of possibilities.

The Bible clearly illustrates that God thrills to do things that seem impossible to man. Scripture tells of his giving sight to the blind and strength to the lame, raising people from the dead, causing barren women to bear children, healing the hopelessly diseased, parting raging rivers, defeating mighty armies, and bringing down the walls of heavily fortified cities.

Yet these instances have one characteristic in common—before a miracle occurred, somebody took God at his word. Somebody refused to acknowledge the impossible. Somebody had faith that with God, the impossible would be possible.

The LORD will hold your hand, and if you
stumble, you still won't fall.
—Psalm 37:24 NASB

96

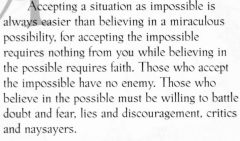

A Moment to Reflect

Accepting a situation as impossible is always easier than believing in a miraculous possibility, for accepting the impossible requires nothing from you while believing in the possible requires faith. Those who accept the impossible have no enemy. Those who believe in the possible must be willing to battle doubt and fear, lies and discouragement, critics and naysayers.

Are there situations in your life that have seemed hopeless? Have you given God any chance to work in ways you cannot work, any chance to do things you cannot do? Recognize today that literally nothing is impossible with God. Claim that truth for your life just now. Choose to believe God for something you cannot accomplish on your own.

Doubt sees the obstacles,
Faith sees the way;
Doubt sees the blackest night,
Faith sees the day;
Doubt dreads to take a step,
Faith soars on high;
Doubt questions,"Who believes?"
Faith answers,"I!"

—Author Unknown

Jesus said, "What is impossible with men is possible with God."

Luke 18:27

A Moment to Refresh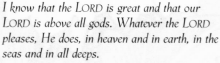

I know that the LORD is great and that our LORD is above all gods. Whatever the LORD pleases, He does, in heaven and in earth, in the seas and in all deeps.

Psalm 135:5–6 NASB

Ah, Sovereign LORD, you have made the heavens and the earth by your great power and outstretched arm. Nothing is too hard for you.

Jeremiah 32:17

Jesus said, "Everything is possible for him who believes."

Mark 9:23

People may plan all kinds of things, but the LORD's will is going to be done.

Proverbs 19:21 GNT

Nothing is impossible with God.

Luke 1:37

*Faith does not operate in the realm of the possible.
There is no glory for God in that which is humanly
possible. Faith begins where man's power ends.*

—GEORGE MÜLLER

*I am the LORD, the God of all mankind. Is
anything too hard for me?*

Jeremiah 32:27

*Jesus saw a fig tree by the side of the road
and went to it, but found nothing on it
except leaves. So he said to the tree, "You
will never again bear fruit!" At once the fig
tree dried up. The disciples saw this and
were astounded. "How did the fig tree dry
up so quickly?" they asked. Jesus answered,
"I assure you that if you believe and do not
doubt, you will be able to do what I have
done to this fig tree. And not only this, but
you will even be able to say to this hill,
'Get up and throw yourself in the sea,' and
it will. If you believe, you will receive
whatever you ask for in prayer."*

Matthew 21:18–22 GNT

*Faith sees the
invisible, believes the
unbelievable, and
receives the
impossible.*

—CORRIE TEN BOOM

99

The Power of Memory

A Moment to Pause

Pause today and recall your favorite moments spent with family. Peruse the memories within an old family photo album or your child's baby book and enjoy the powerful feelings of love, joy, and security they bring. Perhaps these feelings demonstrate why God encourages his children to recall past encounters with him. God realizes you possess a memory of the soul, and your memory has the power to influence your todays as well as your tomorrows.

Memory has the power to dispel fear and impart peace. When you remember God's past dealings with you—the deliverances he provided, the promises he fulfilled, the unexpected joys he freely gave—you cannot be easily haunted by fear. The past becomes a prophet of the future and assures you that God's delivering power, his faithfulness, and his loving-kindness remain forever the same. Why would you fear a future enemy as if God had never empowered you to defeat a foe?

Memory also has the power to establish your confidence. Memories of God's faithfulness give you a confidence based not in hope alone, but also in fact. Keeping memories of God close to your heart enables you to take each next step of life's journey with greater ease and assuredness.

God gave us memories so we could have
roses in the winter.
—Author Unknown

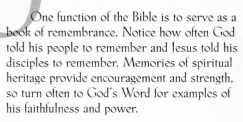

A Moment to Reflect One function of the Bible is to serve as a book of remembrance. Notice how often God told his people to remember and Jesus told his disciples to remember. Memories of spiritual heritage provide encouragement and strength, so turn often to God's Word for examples of his faithfulness and power.

Just as you gather photos and other tokens to help you remember family events, begin also to collect memories of God's power in your life. Perhaps you can keep a journal of special times with the Lord. You may want to mark favorite verses of Scripture in your Bible. Any moment when God is near is a moment you can treasure and reflect upon when you are discouraged or afraid.

The way to enrich life is to keep a retentive memory in the heart. Look over a period of twenty years, and see the all-covering and ever-shining mercy of God! We should lay up some memory of the Divine triumphs which have gladdened our lives, and fall back upon it for inspiration and courage in the dark and cloudy day.

—JOSEPH PARKER

I remember the days of long ago; I meditate on all your works and consider what your hands have done.

Psalm 143:5

A Moment to Refresh

Look to the LORD and his strength; seek his face always. Remember the wonders he has done, his miracles, and the judgments he pronounced.

1 Chronicles 16:11–12

Jesus took bread, gave thanks and broke it, and gave it to the disciples, saying, "This is my body given for you; do this in remembrance of me."

Luke 22:19

I will remember the deeds of the Lord; yes, I will remember your miracles of long ago. I will meditate on all your works and consider all your mighty deeds. Your ways, O God, are holy. What god is so great as our God? You are the God who performs miracles; you display your power among the peoples.

Psalm 77:11–14

When you hold close your memories with God, the power of circumstance is nullified.

❧

—Melinda Mahand

The Counselor, the Holy Spirit, whom the Father will send in my name, will teach you all things and will remind you of everything I have said to you.

John 14:26

Praise the LORD, O my soul, and forget not all his benefits—who forgives all your sins and heals all your diseases, who redeems your life from the pit and crowns you with love and compassion, who satisfies your desires with good things so that your youth is renewed like the eagle's.

Psalm 103:2–5

This I recall to my mind, Therefore I have hope. The Lord's lovingkindnesses indeed never cease, for His compassions never fail. They are new every morning; great is Your faithfulness.

Lamentations 3:21–23 NASB

To live is to remember and to remember is to live.

❧

—Samuel Butler

Obedience Is Rewarded

A Moment to Pause

Treat yourself to a few minutes of quiet reflection today. Consider what part obedience plays in the relationships of your life and what the various benefits of obedience are within each one. For instance, you are in relationship with other members of society. When you obey society's laws, you enjoy the benefit of freedom and all its privileges. If you are employed, your obedience to company guidelines results in a salary and perhaps even a promotion or raise. As a parent, you know your obedient child merits increased responsibilities and privileges. Likewise, when you are in relationship with God, your obedience to him brings many rewards.

Sometimes, however, the idea of God desiring obedience may cause your independent spirit to bristle. You may feel God is relegating you to a demeaning position. Yet the incredible truth is that obedience elevates you to be a fellow worker with God. By desiring to know and do the will of God, you actually link yourself to the whole of God's providence.

As a participator in God's work, you receive added benefits as well. Just a few benefits that Scripture names are answered prayer, long life on earth, eternal life in heaven, God's blessing, and God's protection.

All heaven is waiting to help those who will
discover the will of God and do it.
—J. Robert Ashcroft

A Moment to Reflect

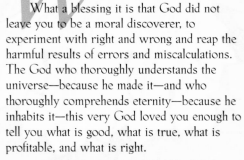

What a blessing it is that God did not leave you to be a moral discoverer, to experiment with right and wrong and reap the harmful results of errors and miscalculations. The God who thoroughly understands the universe—because he made it—and who thoroughly comprehends eternity—because he inhabits it—this very God loved you enough to tell you what is good, what is true, what is profitable, and what is right.

Recognize that a true spirit of obedience is not the result of force but merely of a loving heart's consent. God must have a spirit in tune with his own purposes. Will your response of love today be obedience?

If two angels were to receive at the same moment a commission from God, one to go down and rule earth's grandest empire, the other to go and sweep the streets of its meanest village, it would be a matter of entire indifference to each which service fell to his lot, the post of ruler or the post of scavenger; for the joy of the angels lies only in obedience to God's will.

—JOHN NEWTON

Does the LORD delight in burnt offerings and sacrifices as much as in obeying the voice of the LORD? To obey is better than sacrifice, and to heed is better than the fat of rams.

1 Samuel 15:22

A Moment to Refresh

Jesus said, "If you love me, you will obey what I command. And I will ask the Father, and he will give you another Counselor to be with you forever—the Spirit of truth."

John 14:15–17

Be ye doers of the word, and not hearers only, deceiving your own selves.... But whoso looketh into the perfect law of liberty, and continueth therein, he being not a forgetful hearer, but a doer of the work, this man shall be blessed in his deed.

James 1:22, 25 KJV

Our Father in heaven, hallowed be your name. Your kingdom come. Your will be done, on earth as it is in heaven.

Matthew 6:9–10 NRSV

The strength and happiness of a man is finding out the way in which God is going, and going that way too.

๛

—HENRY WARD BEECHER

I desire to do your will, O my God; your law is within my heart.

Psalm 40:8

Once made perfect, Jesus became the source of eternal salvation for all who obey him.

Hebrews 5:9

Teach me, O LORD, to follow your decrees; then I will keep them to the end. Give me understanding, and I will keep your law and obey it with all my heart. Direct me in the path of your commands, for there I find delight.

Psalm 119:33–35

The world and its desires pass away, but the man who does the will of God lives forever.

1 John 2:17

By obeying Christ's commands, you will gain more than you can give.

๛

—THOMAS BROOKS

The Search for Truth

A Moment to Pause

Search today for a time and place to be alone with God for a while. Once you are comfortably settled, think about how much time each day you spend simply searching. How often do you search for a phone number, your child's misplaced toy, your car in a parking lot, or some item in the recesses of the refrigerator? While in the process of these searches, you are totally preoccupied with the endeavor. You think of nothing else. Yet throughout life, people are continually on a far more important search that often takes place on a subconscious level. This search is the search for truth.

Truth is not as elusive as we sometimes think. Consider, for example, that a gemologist learns to recognize a true diamond by studying the traits of a true diamond. In this way the gemologist becomes familiar with what is true. This familiarity with truth allows the gemologist to recognize any deception, any falsehood, anything less than a true gem.

So it is with truth. One does not discover truth by examining every falsehood. One learns to recognize truth by examining truth, and the place to begin discovering truth is in the person of Jesus.

I have chosen the way of truth; I have set my heart on your laws.... I run in the path of your commands, for you have set my heart free.
—Psalm 119:30, 32

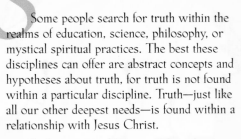

A Moment to Reflect

S

Some people search for truth within the realms of education, science, philosophy, or mystical spiritual practices. The best these disciplines can offer are abstract concepts and hypotheses about truth, for truth is not found within a particular discipline. Truth—just like all our other deepest needs—is found within a relationship with Jesus Christ.

In the person of Jesus, you have been given a living example of truth. Jesus' principles and ways are true. His love is true, and his message is true. In addition, God has provided a book of truth, the Bible.

If your heart longs for truth today, spend some time reading about Jesus in Scripture. Perhaps the verses on the following pages can serve as a beginning point.

Nothing will stand but truth; truth will stand when all things fail. It lives in the open air all the days of the year; it can go out at midnight as safely as at midday; it speaks to a king, to a child, to a peasant, with all the simplicity of innocence and the beauteousness of a high and noble and valiant courage.

—JOSEPH PARKER

The LORD is the true God;
he is the living God, the eternal King.

Jeremiah 10:10

A Moment to Refresh

Jesus said, "If you hold to my teaching, you are
really my disciples. Then you will know the
truth, and the truth will set you free."

John 8:31–32

All your words are true; all your righteous
laws are eternal.... I hate and abhor falsehood
but I love your law. Seven times a day I praise
you for your righteous laws. Great peace have
they who love your law, and nothing can make
them stumble.

Psalm 119:160, 163–165

Do not let kindness and truth leave you; bind
them around your neck, write them on the tablet
of your heart. So you will find favor and good
repute in the sight of God and man.

Proverbs 3:3–4 NASB

*What God's Son has told me, take for true I do; Truth himself
speaks truly or there's nothing true.*

༄

—THOMAS AQUINAS

*Jesus said, "I am the way and the truth and
the life. No one comes to the Father except
through me."*

John 14:6

*You also were included in Christ when you
heard the word of truth, the gospel of your
salvation. Having believed, you were
marked in him with a seal, the promised
Holy Spirit.*

Ephesians 1:13

*When he, the Spirit of truth, comes, he will
guide you into all truth.*

John 16:13

*The law was given through Moses; grace
and truth came through Jesus Christ.*

John 1:17

*The desire for truth
is the desire for God.*

༄

—JOHN MACQUARRIE

God's Secret

A Moment to Pause

Do you enjoy secrets? Recall for a moment that special feeling of delight you experienced the last time someone shared a secret surprise with you. Then bend close to hear, for God too has shared a great secret. Tucked away within the pages of Scripture lies the surprising revelation that the most valuable possession on earth is not gold, silver, or rubies, not honor, strength, or power. Rather, the most valuable possession is the unassuming quality of wisdom.

Wisdom's value is no more a secret than any other of God's truths. The declarations regarding wisdom are contained within God's Word for all to read. This one truth is rarely taken at face value.

Perhaps part of the hesitation is that wisdom is believed to be a trait that people just naturally do or do not have. Once again, God has a great surprise. Wisdom is not simply a part of some people's nature. Wisdom is a trait any of God's children can acquire simply by asking. In fact, God actually *wants* you to ask. The Bible relates that when Solomon asked for wisdom, God was so pleased that he blessed Solomon not only with wisdom, but also with wealth and honor.

Wisdom is better than rubies; and all the things that may be desired are not to be compared with it.
—*Proverbs 8:11 KJV*

How do you picture wisdom? Do you imagine a studious professor wearing glasses and chalk dust? Do you visualize a feeble, old man sitting on a mountain, aloof and ineffectual? Begin today to change your mental image. The book of Proverbs in the Bible describes wisdom as a woman. She is powerful and strong, capable and confident, valuable and prized. She instructs, she blesses, and she protects. Certainly that image is much more effective in helping you understand wisdom's true value and inspiring you to seek it!

Today may your first act be to ask God for wisdom. May your second act be to look for wisdom within the pages of God's Word. The book of Proverbs is a great place to start.

If you are wise you will show yourself rather as a reservoir than a canal. For a canal spreads abroad the water it receives, but a reservoir waits until it is filled before overflowing, and this shares without loss to itself its super-abundance of water.

—BERNARD OF CLAIRVAUX

A wise man is strong; yea, a man of knowledge increaseth strength.

Proverbs 24:5 KJV

A Moment to Refresh

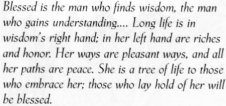

Blessed is the man who finds wisdom, the man who gains understanding.... Long life is in wisdom's right hand; in her left hand are riches and honor. Her ways are pleasant ways, and all her paths are peace. She is a tree of life to those who embrace her; those who lay hold of her will be blessed.

Proverbs 3:13, 16–18

Wisdom is as good as an inheritance, an advantage to those who see the sun. For the protection of wisdom is like the protection of money, and the advantage of knowledge is that wisdom gives life to the one who possesses it.

Ecclesiastes 7:11–12 NRSV

The fear of the LORD is the beginning of wisdom; all those who practice it have a good understanding. His praise endures forever.

Psalm 111:10 NRSV

Wisdom is the ability to use knowledge so as to meet successfully the emergencies of life. Men may acquire knowledge, but wisdom is a gift direct from God.

—Bob Jones

How much better to get wisdom than gold, to choose understanding rather than silver.
Proverbs 16:16

The wisdom that comes from heaven is first of all pure; then peace-loving, considerate, submissive, full of mercy and good fruit, impartial and sincere.
James 3:17

The law of the LORD is perfect, reviving the soul. The statutes of the LORD are trustworthy, making wise the simple. The precepts of the LORD are right, giving joy to the heart. The commands of the Lord are radiant, giving light to the eyes.
Psalm 19:7–8

Surely the essence of wisdom is that before we begin to act at all, or attempt to please God, we should discover what it is that God has to say about the matter.

—D. Martin Lloyd-Jones

One Who Is Faithful

A Moment to Pause

Treat yourself today to a time of comfort for body and soul. Curl up in your favorite cozy place and enjoy thinking of someone you love. Try to choose a word that describes that person's character. You will probably find it an interesting endeavor to distill your loved one's character into a single word. The Bible, however, has the unique challenge of describing the very character of God. If you considered all the descriptions that Scripture provides and tried to distill God's character into only one word, the best choice would be the word *faithful*.

At first you might disagree with the choice of *faithful* and propose that the word *loving* or *powerful* or *forgiving* would be better. Without faithfulness, any other descriptions would be unreliable. They would be meaningless because they would be momentary. Faithfulness is what causes the God you know today to be the same God you will know tomorrow.

God's faithfulness is, in essence, the very foundation of his character. Without it, other descriptions are mere sentiment, susceptible to being changed by time and circumstance.

Without faithfulness, the thought of eternity would be terrifying. Because God is faithful, you are secure.

Though men are false, God is faithful.
—Matthew Henry

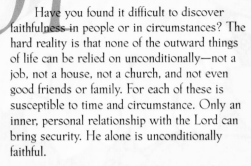

A Moment to Reflect

Have you found it difficult to discover faithfulness in people or in circumstances? The hard reality is that none of the outward things of life can be relied on unconditionally—not a job, not a house, not a church, and not even good friends or family. For each of these is susceptible to time and circumstance. Only an inner, personal relationship with the Lord can bring security. He alone is unconditionally faithful.

Know today that God's love toward you, his strength in you, his protection over you, and his provision for you will never falter. Trust him though all else seems unsettled and insecure. His faithfulness will be the one thing by which you can define and purpose your life.

Morning by morning new mercies I see;
All I have needed Thy hand hath provided—
Great is Thy faithfulness, Lord, unto me!

—*Thomas O. Chisholm*

117

God, who has called you into fellowship with
his Son Jesus Christ our Lord, is faithful.
1 Corinthians 1:9

A Moment to Refresh

Your love, O LORD, reaches to the heavens,
your faithfulness to the skies. Your
righteousness is like the mighty mountains, your
justice like the great deep. O LORD, you
preserve both man and beast.

Psalm 36:5–6

I saw heaven opened, and there was a white
horse! Its rider is called Faithful and True, and
in righteousness he judges and makes war....
On his robe and on his thigh he has a name
inscribed, "King of kings and Lord of lords."
Revelation 19:11, 16 NRSV

Know therefore that the LORD your God is
God; he is the faithful God, keeping his
covenant of love to a thousand generations of
those who love him and keep his commands.
Deuteronomy 7:9

In God's faithfulness lies eternal security.

—Corrie ten Boom

If we are faithless, Jesus will remain faithful, for he cannot disown himself.
2 Timothy 2:13

O Lord, You are my God; I will exalt you and praise your name, for in perfect faithfulness you have done marvelous things, things planned long ago.
Isaiah 25:1

The Lord is faithful, and He will strengthen and protect you.
2 Thessalonians 3:3

I will proclaim the name of the Lord. Oh, praise the greatness of our God! He is the Rock, his works are perfect, and all his ways are just. A faithful God who does no wrong, upright and just is he.
Deuteronomy 32:3–4

Change and decay in all around I see; O thou, who changest not, abide with me.

—Henry Francis Lyte

The Presence of Peace

A Moment to Pause

In a household of busy children and hectic schedules, finding a moment of peace and quiet can be quite a challenge. Sometimes, in fact, the only place you can find peace is within the inner recesses of your soul. Retreat to that place of inner rest today as you consider the essence of true peace.

Sometimes people think of peace as being the absence of war, affliction, or adversity. True peace is not the absence of something, but rather the presence of something—the presence of God within one's soul. God's inner presence enables you to walk assuredly through the ever-changing circumstances of life. Even when you are outwardly in trouble, inwardly you can possess an unfailing peace, a consistent confidence in God, his power, and his resources.

The world seems to live in a constant state of unrest, at the mercy of what is called chance or misfortune. As God's child, you walk in peace through the midst of a storm and, therefore, cause the world to wonder. You become a living example of a spiritual dimension that overcomes the temporal. This example opens the door for you to tell others of the God whose presence promises peace.

A peaceable man does more good than a learned one.
—Thomas à Kempis

A Moment to Reflect

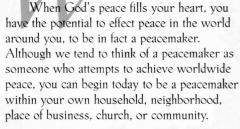

When God's peace fills your heart, you have the potential to effect peace in the world around you, to be in fact a peacemaker. Although we tend to think of a peacemaker as someone who attempts to achieve worldwide peace, you can begin today to be a peacemaker within your own household, neighborhood, place of business, church, or community.

Is there a troubled spirit you can soothe? Is there a disagreement you can mediate? Is there a brewing storm you can calm? Keep your eyes open for such an opportunity today. For peace, even if brought only to one heart or to one home, is a great blessing.

Lord, make me an instrument of your peace. Where there is hatred, let me sow love. Where there is injury, pardon. Where there is discord, vision. Where there is doubt, faith. Where there is despair, hope. Where there is darkness, light. Where there is sadness, joy.

—Francis of Assisi

*Blessed are the peacemakers: for they shall be
called the children of God.*

Matthew 5:9 KJV

A Moment to Refresh

*Peacemakers who sow in peace raise a harvest
of righteousness.*

James 3:18

*How wonderful it is to see a messenger coming
across the mountains, bringing good news, the
news of peace!*

Isaiah 52:7 GNT

*The fruit of the Spirit is love, joy, peace,
patience, kindness, goodness, faithfulness,
gentleness and self-control. Against such things
there is no law.*

Galatians 5:22–23

*The LORD gives strength to his people; the
LORD blesses his people with peace.*

Psalm 29:11

Reconciliation is not weakness or cowardice. It demands courage, mobility, generosity, sometimes heroism, an overcoming of oneself rather than of one's adversary.

—PAUL VI

Consider the blameless, observe the upright; there is a future for the man of peace.

Psalm 37:37

The LORD bless thee, and keep thee: The LORD make his face shine upon thee, and be gracious unto thee: The LORD lift up his countenance upon thee, and give thee peace.

Numbers 6:24–26 KJV

When a man's ways please the LORD, he maketh even his enemies to be at peace with him.

Proverbs 16:7 KJV

No God, no peace. Know God, know peace.

—AUTHOR UNKNOWN

A Position of Praise

A Moment to Pause
How has God blessed you today? Has he lifted your spirits through the smile of your child? Has he supplied an answer to prayer? Has he sent the encouragement of a friend? Spend a few moments just now remembering recent blessings and praising God for each one.

The Bible puts emphatic importance on God's people praising him. Two of the most apparent reasons are that God deserves praise and that praise pleases him. Praise is crucial to the life of a Christian for another reason as well. The fact is that praise is one of the most incredible avenues God has given for you to know him and to release his power to work on your behalf.

Praise puts you in a position to focus on the attributes of God, his work in your life, and his goodness toward you. This position automatically gives you an intimate awareness of who God is and how much he cares for you. In turn, this knowledge of his loving care provides you assurance and power to face the day. Finally, your acknowledgment and appreciation of God motivates him to continue his work in your life.

Praise is given to God, but the blessings come back to you.

There is nothing that pleases the Lord so much as praise.
—Author Unknown

Sometimes the word *praise* can be frightening. People are not exactly sure what it is or how to do it. Praise is simply adoring God and declaring back to him the truth about who he is and what he does. There are no special words to use or positions to be in. Praise is just your heart talking to God's heart about his wonderful attributes and actions.

Will you take time to praise God today? Through praise, you take your eyes off your problems and focus instead on God. There in his presence you find hope, help, and healing. For once again, praise is given to God, but the blessings come back to you.

*If any one would tell you the shortest, surest way
to all happiness and all perfection he must tell
you to make it a rule to yourself to thank and
praise God for everything that happens to you.
For it is certain that whatever seeming calamity
happens to you, if you thank and praise God for
it, you turn it into a blessing.*

— WILLIAM LAW

I will praise you, O LORD, with all my heart; I will tell of all your wonders. I will be glad and rejoice in you; I will sing praise to your name, O Most High.

Psalm 9:1–2

A Moment to Refresh

I will bless the LORD at all times: his praise shall continually be in my mouth. My soul shall make her boast in the LORD: the humble shall hear thereof, and be glad. O magnify the LORD with me, and let us exalt his name together.

Psalm 34:1–3 KJV

The LORD is my strength and my song; he has become my salvation. He is my God, and I will praise him, my father's God, and I will exalt him.... Who among the gods is like you, O LORD? Who is like you—majestic in holiness, awesome in glory, working wonders?... The LORD will reign for ever and ever.

Exodus 15:2, 11, 18

Through Jesus, therefore, let us continually offer to God a sacrifice of praise—the fruit of lips that confess his name. And do not forget to do good and to share with others, for with such sacrifices God is pleased.

Hebrews 13:15–16

In prayer we act like men; in praise we act like angels.

—THOMAS WATSON

Wealth and honor come from you; you are the ruler of all things. In your hands are strength and power to exalt and give strength to all. Now, our God, we give you thanks, and praise your glorious name.

1 Chronicles 29:12–13

Shout for joy to the LORD, all the earth. Worship the LORD with gladness; come before him with joyful songs. Know that the LORD is God. It is he who made us, and we are his; we are his people, the sheep of his pasture. Enter his gates with thanksgiving and his courts with praise; give thanks to him and praise his name. For the LORD is good and his love endures forever; his faithfulness continues through all generations.

Psalm 100:1–5

There is more healing joy in five minutes of worship than there is in five nights of revelry.

—A. W. TOZER

Other books in the Soul Retreats™ series:

Soul Retreats™ for Busy People
Soul Retreats™ for Teachers
Soul Retreats™ for Women

All available from your favorite bookstore.
We would like to hear from you.
Please send your comments about this book to:

Inspirio™, *the gift group of Zondervan*
Attn: Product Development
Grand Rapids, Michigan 49530
www.inspirio.com

<u>Our mission:</u>
To produce distinctively Christian gifts that point people to God's Word
with refreshing messages and innovative designs.

inspirio™